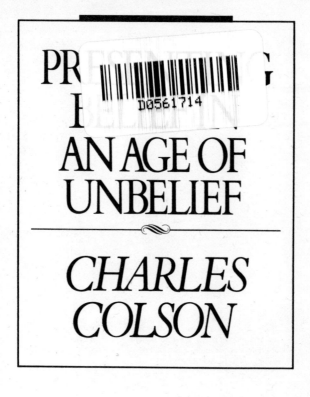

PRESENTING BELIEF IN AN AGE OF UNBELIEF

CHARLES COLSON

VICTOR BOOKS a division of SP Publications, Inc.
WHEATON. ILLINOIS 60187

Offices also in
Whitby, Ontario, Canada
Amersham-on-the-Hill, Bucks, England

Prison Fellowship Ministries
P.O. Box 17500
Washington, D.C. 20041

Presenting Belief in an Age of Unbelief is based on Charles Colson's speech at the Evangelical Press Association convention, Washington, D.C., May 1984.

Back cover photography by David Singer.

Recommended Dewey Decimal Classification: 269
Suggested Subject Heading: SPIRITUAL RENEWAL
ISBN: 0-89693-158-7

VICTOR BOOKS
A division of SP Publications, Inc.
Wheaton, Illinois 60187

The

CHALLENGING THE CHURCH
Series
by
CHARLES COLSON

Dare to Be Different, Dare to Be Christian

Presenting Belief in an Age of Unbelief

The Role of the Church in Society

The Struggle for Men's Hearts and Minds

INTRODUCTION

We live in a time that would seem to be marked by unprecedented spiritual resurgence: 96 percent of all Americans say they believe in God; 80 percent profess to be Christians.

Yet families are splitting apart in record numbers. Countless millions of unborn children have been murdered since 1973. And there are 100 times more burglaries in so-called "Christian" America than in so-called "pagan" Japan.

Why this paradox between profession and practice? Why is the faith of more than 50 million Americans who claim to be born again not making more of an impact on the moral values of our land?

The answer is what Dietrich Bonhoeffer, the German pastor martyred by the Nazis, labeled cheap grace: the perception that Christianity offers only a flood of blessings, the rights of the kingdom without responsibilities to the King. This easy believism fails to take biblical truth to heart and fails to act in obedience to the Scriptures. The result is a church which increasingly accommodates secular values. Not knowingly, of course, but simply by gradual acceptance of secular standards which have become comfortable.

We needn't fear a sinister conspiracy to impose atheism on our society. Though such forces may be at work, they will fail precisely because they are overt.

No, the real peril today comes from the subtle ways in which the mind of our culture is being gradually won over to secular values—in the media, in classrooms, and tragically, even in our church pews. This threat is all the more insidious because it is unseen. It is the cancer of compromise.

God is calling His people today to challenge secular values, measuring them in the light of biblical revelation. Will we cave in to a culture which in principle and practice denies Christ's lordship, or will we heed His call and stand for Him?

Doing so will put us in sharp conflict with much of what the world exalts, but that must be our witness. Two centuries ago, John Wesley wrote, "Making an open stand against all ungodliness and unrighteousness, which overspreads our land as a flood, is one of the noblest ways of confessing Christ in the face of His enemies."

I can think of no more timely challenge for the Christian church today.

PRESENTING BELIEF IN AN AGE OF UNBELIEF

For more than 30 years each technological advance and expansion of government power was measured against the vision of George Orwell's extraordinary novel *1984.*

Now, in retrospect, the judgment of most commentators has been nearly unanimous: Orwell, sick and disillusioned with the vain promise of Socialist utopia, was overly pessimistic. He underestimated the strength of the West economically and politically, failed to reckon with the human spirit, and as a struggling agnostic, could not anticipate the work of a sovereign God in history. There has been no "Big Brother" or "newspeak" (at least not in the obvious form Orwell pictured), no tele-screens or thought control. We have escaped those dire predictions—so far. But have we really?

There is, I believe, a profound insight buried in Orwell's exaggerated satire. It is captured in this description of Winston Smith's reflections: "It struck him [Orwell] that the truly characteristic thing about modern life was not its cruelty and insecurity but simply its bareness, its dinginess, its listlessness." Later Smith continues, "Orthodoxy means not thinking, not needing to think; orthodoxy is unconsciousness."

The Sin of Our Times

If we are honest, it would be difficult to find a more accurate characterization of our times. And if we are honest, we are forced to admit that what only a tyrannical Big Brother could accomplish in Orwell's *1984,* our self-indulgent Western society has very nearly managed to do to itself today. Of course, our seduction has been more subtle and therefore far more insidious— through the influences of mass media and advertising, the relentless pursuit of hedonism, and the unthinking, uncritical acceptance of prevailing and declining moral and educational values.

We have, to an alarming degree, become victims of our own mindless conformity—self-absorbed, indifferent, empty of heart, the "hollow men" that T.S. Eliot wrote about in the early part of the century. Yes, orthodoxy has become unconsciousness; nihilism is the spirit of this spiritless age.

A tragic example of this was the accidental death of David Kennedy, the fourth son of the late Senator Robert Kennedy. Kennedy, 28, was found dead in a Palm Beach, Florida hotel room, apparently the victim of a drug overdose.

Referring to David's struggle with drug addiction, a grieving friend reported to *The Washington Post,* "In David's case, there was nothing to connect to in life. Even free of the drug influence, there was a deep, overpowering sense of nihilism in his personality. No person, no job, no hobby could give him something to plug into."

Dorothy Sayers, the astute contemporary of C.S. Lewis, said the sin of our times is "the sin that believes in nothing, cares for nothing, seeks to know nothing, interferes with nothing, enjoys nothing, hates nothing, finds purpose in nothing, lives for nothing, and remains alive because there is nothing for which it will die."

Totalitarianism is not the

conquering tyrant, enslaving us to the state; it is nihilism. We have yielded to the insidious enslavement of self-gratification. The villain, in short, is us.

Too extreme a view, you say? Consider just these few manifestations:

- In the name of the "right" of a woman to control her own body, 1.5 million unborn children were murdered in America in 1983. More humans have been disposed of in this country since the legalization of abortion in 1973 than during the Holocaust in World War II. Who, I might ask, has inflicted a more widespread tyranny—Hitler, a maniacal dictator, or an uncaring, indifferent society? Sure, a few "religious fanatics" rant and rave, but most people are unmoved. Orthodoxy has become unconsciousness.

- As a society, we have believed Socrates, that sin is the result of ignorance, and Hegel, that man is evolving through increasing knowledge to superior moral levels. And so we've done away with any sense of individual responsibility.

What delusions! In this, the most educated and advanced society the world has ever known, we have a divorce rate which until 1983 had increased steadily for 20 years, soaring crime rates, widespread child abuse, and countless shattered families. A valueless culture breeds the most awful tyranny.

- As a nation we have been blessed with unprecedented material abundance; but what it has produced is a boredom so pervasive that drug use is epidemic. I was recently with an extremely successful businessman, a great entrepreneur whose name you would immediately know. He told me excitedly that he had discovered a great untapped potential business: drug and alcohol rehabilitation. "It's the fastest growth industry in America, with surefire profits," he told me. So dramatic has been the recent increase in drug and alcohol addiction that our facilities are completely incapable of handling the casualties.

- And nowhere is the abandonment of responsibility more evident than in our inability—or unwillingness—to form a humanitarian consensus in foreign policy. Few seem to care if other nations, even our neighbors to the south, are swallowed up by totalitarian forces. Our isolationism, I must add, in some measure results from disillusionment with Vietnam and from the activism of sincere pacifists; but for the most part it is simply a manifestation of the selfishness of a culture which cares only to look out for number one.

The obsessive egocentricity of secular culture today—Scott Peck calls it "narcissism" in his book *People of the Lie*—creates a special tyranny of its own. Like the young woman cited in a *Psychology Today* magazine article, her nerves shot from too many all-night parties, her life an endless round of pot, booze, and sex. When asked by a therapist, "Why don't you stop?" her startled reply was, "You mean I really don't have to do what I want to do?"

Who is the tyrant in our hedonistic society? Not Big Brother. Us.

The Church in Trouble

But the most frightening fact of our world today is that the church of Jesus Christ is in almost as much trouble as the culture. Unthinkingly, we have almost completely bought into the counterfeit secular value system. In fact, we can one-up it, since God is on our side. Unfortunately, this skewed Gospel and cheap grace are what prevent the church from making any real impact for Christ.

Many Christians attribute our impotence to the fact that we are being overrun by the culture, victimized by the media; that the reason we can't get our message across to the secular world is because we are thwarted by those who control the all-powerful tube. And there's a lot of truth to this. But there is another side. When once I was with the president of one of the television networks, I chided him for not putting more wholesome family programming on prime-time television. And since Gallup polls show that one third of all Americans claim to be born again, I told him he was missing a good market by not airing more shows with Christian values.

"Oh," he replied, "You mean like *Chariots of Fire?*"

"Yes," I exclaimed. "I've seen it 10 times. I think it's one of the most powerful penetrations of the Gospel into the arts in this generation."

"Well," he said, "CBS ran *Chariots of Fire* as its Sunday Night Movie some months ago. That same night NBC had *On Golden Pond* and ABC had *My Mother's Secret Life*—a soap opera about a mother who was hiding her past as a prostitute. Let me tell you the ratings. *On Golden Pond* was number 1, with 25.2 percent of all TV sets in America tuned in. *My Mother's Secret Life* drew a rating of 25.1 percent. Way in the distance, losing its shirt was CBS with *Chariots of Fire*—11.8 percent. Of the 65 shows rated that week 'Dallas' was number 1, *Chariots of Fire* number 57."

Then he looked at me smugly and asked, "So where, Mr. Colson, are your 50 million born-again Christians?" I had no answer. Where are we?

You see, in *1984*—the novel, that is—the instrument by which Big Brother controlled people was the telescreen. He saw everything; if they looked back into the telescreen they saw Big Brother. But when *we* look into the television set we see something much more terrifying than the image of Big Brother. We see ourselves. Television is but a mirror reflection. Orthodoxy has become unconsciousness.

Alexander Solzhenitsyn, the Nobel laureate whom I consider one of the greatest prophetic voices of God today, captured the dilemma of our times brilliantly in his speech accepting the Templeton Prize for the Advancement of Religion. He recalled during his childhood in Russia that when great disasters came, people would respond, "Men have forgotten God. That's why all this has happened." And in his survey of 20th-century Western culture, Solzhenitsyn could find nothing better to describe what has happened than that pithy Russian proverb, "Men have forgotten God."

The great drama of our day is deeper than Communism versus capitalism, totalitarianism versus democracy, or East versus West. The real struggle is belief versus unbelief.

Is Carl Sagan's creed, which is taught in our schools, correct that "the Cosmos is all there is or ever will be," or is there a sovereign God who manifests Himself in His Word and in the person of Jesus Christ, the same yesterday, today, and forever? That's the great battle—and it's uphill.

The Challenge of Change

So the great question for us, as evangelical Christians, charged with making disciples of all nations, is how to fulfill our biblical commission in such a time as this, bringing meaning to a culture wallowing in meaninglessness.

How *do* we present a message of belief in an age of unbelief? Charting our course is made all the more challenging when we recognize that the very nature of evangelicalism, evangelism included, as we've known it, is in a time of transition, making some dramatic changes inevitable.

Consider just these four factors of change:

The first is leadership. Over the

past four decades, one man, Billy Graham, has been singularly used of God—quite possibly as the greatest evangelist of all time. I hope Billy will continue preaching for a long, long time—John Wesley did until he was 87. But we evangelicals who have relied so heavily on him must recognize that the day will come when we cannot.

That day will, I believe, also mark the end of the era of stadium mass evangelism—at least in the United States. Billy's unique charisma always generates a sense of expectancy and excitement, but for anyone else, and for almost any other purpose, with each passing year it becomes more difficult to bring thousands into stadiums. There are a host of sociological reasons: crime in urban areas, television, growing public apathy, lack of effective organization, to mention but a few.

In my opinion, when the mantle of leadership is passed, it will fall not to any one individual, but to hundreds, perhaps thousands. One of the most thrilling moments of my Christian life was to see nearly 5,000 evangelists from all over the world in Amsterdam for Billy's first conference for itinerant evangelists in 1983. It is impossible for me to describe the excitement in that auditorium. Men and women from every nation sat furiously taking notes as Billy and others shared their most intimate experiences as evangelists and coached them on how to preach, how to prepare sermons, how to discern the needs of their audience. I hope Billy will do much more of this in the years ahead, and that through this remarkable man God will continue to raise up thousands of disciples to plant the Gospel in every corner of the earth. But we must recognize that evangelism leadership will be diffused—and spread around the world.

The second is the changing nature of the media. As the extraordinary technological breakthroughs of recent years—instant communications, home satellite receivers, and the like—are dramatically changing American habits, so have they begun to change the character of the American evangelist. Modern technology permitted the remarkable growth of Christian television and created new Christian folk heroes almost overnight. So great was the hunger of the evangelical viewer to be affirmed in his own beliefs that funds poured in.

But the honeymoon may soon be over. Television, by its very nature, must provide ever-increasing thrills to hold its audience; otherwise its viewers will just switch channels. And to catch the attention of viewers used to 30-second commercials it has to reduce the Gospel message to simple slogans.

As the novelty of Christian TV wears off, I believe a winnowing process will begin. It may already have. I have talked with TV evangelists who tell me that even in good markets it is becoming difficult to maintain their needed financial support. So many TV evangelists are being forced to plead for funds to remain on the air that airtime for the real message grows less and less.

I hasten to add, however, that quality programming with theological integrity will prosper. Witness the incredible growth of Jim Dobson's outstanding radio series, just to mention one of many examples.

Third, the great charismatic explosion which began more than a decade ago may be tapering off. Traditional evangelicals, by the way, owe much to the charismatic movement for bringing back to the church a sense of the supernatural, of worship, of adoration. But like all movements that begin with great spontaneity, this too is becoming institutionalized and large numbers of charismatics are settling into the mainstream of the church.

Fourth, the process of

"privatization," as Os Guinness calls it, sadly will intensify as society becomes more impersonal and individuals feel more alienated. People will, I fear, continue to compartmentalize their lives including their religious experience. Ask a Christian layperson his ministry and he will inevitably respond, "Gideons on Thursday night," or "Prison Fellowship on Monday night," or "Sunday School." The process of privatization destroys our understanding of ministry which is 24 hours a day, being Christ's person wherever we are, in business, the home, the country club, or the ghetto.

Strategy for Evangelism

These developments should cause us to thoughtfully and prayerfully examine our strategy for evangelism for the balance of this century. In this spirit, let me suggest five areas of challenge and opportunity.

First, authentic evangelism must involve the totality of life. Jesus said, "You *shall* be My witnesses," but a lot of Christians have taken that commandment to mean that we are *to* witness. So we have reduced evangelism to verbal formulas, neat, easy-step plans—just utter these simple phrases and you'll be part of the club.

And some people seem to think that the simpler we can communicate the Gospel, the more people we can recruit. Maybe so, but the question is "recruit them for what?" Millard Fuller of Habitat for Humanity tells the story of his experience in Zaire, where Christians had trained parrots to say, "I love Jesus." Not unfairly, I think Fuller likens many who sit in pews every Sunday morning, mindlessly chanting their creeds, to those parrots.

Packaging the Gospel into tidy packages has some serious dangers. For one thing, it tends to cheapen the message. When we tell the world that all there is to becoming a Christian is a simple prayer—and thereafter God will shower blessings upon them—we are selling the world a false bill of goods. We will pay for it—if not from the angry disillusioned millions to whom we sell our false message, then surely on Judgment Day. Then too, we can easily fall into the snare of turning evangelism into a big game hunt—keeping score and measuring success by the fame and power of our convert trophies.

This is why it is so important to focus on Jesus' command that we *be* witnesses. Jesus means, I believe, that evangelism is to involve the totality of our lives. Everything about our lifestyle counts—how we spend our money, how we treat our children, our business ethics, our political values, our domestic relations, and on and on. (And this means far more than being faithful in church every Sunday morning, or not smoking, drinking, using foul language, or associating with those who do.)

Christians are supposed to be humble, yet we can get caught up in our own importance—and as the evangelical movement burgeons, with our own power. During a press conference at a Christian broadcasters' convention, a reporter from a prominent national daily challenged me, "I don't know what all this born-again business means, but I have been at this convention two days, and everywhere I go, the people I interview seem to think they have all the answers. As a matter of fact, the bigger the exhibit, the more arrogant the individual. Aren't born-again Christians supposed to be loving?"

I defended my brethren, pointing out that most of them enter the ministry for all the best reasons, but that we Christians are not immune to the seduction of power. But I had to bite my lip because I know exactly what that reporter was talking about—and so do you. How we need to be reminded of the oft-quoted adage that "evangelism is like one beggar showing another beggar where he found bread."

Joseph Bayly's book, *The Gospel Blimp*, should be mandatory reading for evangelicals. While we are creating sophisticated organizations and employing the latest technology to win the world to Christ, let us not forget that our neighbor judges Jesus Christ by what he sees in us.

Second, evangelism demands serious discipleship. Our task is not simply to get people to recite certain prayers so we can move on to more fertile fields. We are to help lead them to Christ and then teach them spiritual disciplines and truths so that they truly can become disciples— followers of Christ, and in time teachers themselves. One-on-one ministries like The Navigators will, I believe, become increasingly strategic in the decades ahead.

When I asked Christ into my life, I had never heard of evangelical Christianity. I didn't know the jargon or formulas of the evangelical subculture. If there hadn't been someone to take me by the hand and walk me through the Scriptures, help me to pray, help me to feel comfortable with others, I really wonder where I would be today. Doug Coe discipled me constantly. Harold Hughes, my one-time political enemy, loved me even when most people in my own political party turned their back on me. Al Quie, then a Congressman, offered to go to prison for me. Fred Rhodes took early retirement from government to help me start my ministry. And down through the years there have been men like Carl Henry, Richard Lovelace, R.C. Sproul, Dick Halverson, and others who have given so much of themselves to teach me. Whatever growth I have experienced as a Christian has been in large measure due to the sacrificial commitment of others who were willing to invest themselves in me.

And this kind of evangelism cannot be deterred. Mass evangelism through television could be eliminated tomorrow. In a severe economic crisis funds would dry up; government policies could change; so could media ownership; we could be subjected to oppression in this country that would deny the free proclamation of the Gospel.

But there is no power that can ever stop one-on-one discipleship. It is reported that when the missionaries left China and the Communists took over, the most awful persecution of the church, then estimated at more than 1 million believers, began. Surely, after 30 years of brutal, ruthless persecution, the church would be obliterated; but instead, according to many reports, there are today over 30 million Christians in China.

Third, for effective evangelism we must penetrate the mainstream of thought in secular culture. Much of our Christianity today is, sadly, entertainment for the faithful. We talk in our own language to likeminded friends, and the world is content to let us put on our own show, as long as we don't bother anyone.

But we are meant to bother the world—bother it by presenting a message which convicts people of their sin, which offers an alternative to the hollowness and nihilism of secular life.

To invade the secular mainstream—on their turf—requires great creativity and boldness. It means aggressively reaching out and battling for the hearts and minds of our neighbors.

But we can do it. That's why I was so thrilled with the advertising campaign sponsored by the DeMoss Foundation offering *Power for Living,* a little booklet which magnificently presents the Gospel message. It was offered over secular television and in full-page ads in the *Wall Street Journal, The Washington Post,* and other publications. More than 7 million people responded for information about the Gospel; tens of thousands have come to Christ through that magnificent outreach.

The Christian Broadcasting Network's advertising spots during ABC's showing of *The Day After,* one of the most heavily watched programs in the history of television, was another example. Pat Robertson's tasteful invitation to salvation was right where we Christians ought to be—on the front lines of the battle speaking of hope amid the secular world's portrayal of utter hopelessness.

To invade the secular mainstream also means that Christian writers and others with creative talents must compete in the secular media. We need to infiltrate the newsrooms of *The Washington Post* and the *New York Times,* of CBS, ABC, and NBC. We need Christian influence in the arts and music so that God's truth becomes evident in every walk of life.

In that same vein, Christian scholars and thinkers need to do battle with secular intellects. I realize that many Christians believe that reason and faith are incompatible. But that is nonsense. Augustine said, "Believe that you may understand, understand that you may believe."

Let's face it, friends, if we fail to articulate the reasoned defense of our faith, all of our witnessing, plans of salvation, and evangelistic efforts will be for naught. Secularization of Western culture is undermining the presuppositions absolutely essential for effective evangelization. In a society that has lost a common belief in moral absolutes, relativism reigns— thus the Bible is just another book and Jesus simply another superior teacher.

Back to Basics

Fourth, the role of the church in evangelism must be strengthened. In our well-intentioned zeal to win the whole world for Christ, we have tended to concentrate on grand crusades and in the process we often diminish the responsibility of the local church. This is one of the reasons that many churches have become nothing more than Sunday morning civic clubs, places where people go for their one-hour-a-week inspirational fix.

We have allowed ourselves to drift a long way from the biblical vision of the church. Listen to how Aristides described the early church to Hadrian the Roman Emperor: "They love one another, they never fail to help widows, they save orphans from those who would hurt them. If they have something they give freely to the man who has nothing. If they see a stranger they take him home, and are happy as though he were a real brother.

They don't consider themselves brothers in the usual sense, but brothers instead through the Spirit, in God."

That is evangelism, when people *see* God's power lived as a new order, their values in sharp contrast to the ways of the world. That's making the "invisible kingdom visible," as John Calvin put it.

The success of evangelism in the next decade, I am convinced, will be in direct proportion to the strength of the local church. But because we have failed to make the church all that it is supposed to be, the culture doesn't expect much from it; in fact, it's so unaccustomed to our asserting our biblical responsibilities that when we do, the culture recoils in surprise and then fights back.

For example, in Collinsville, Oklahoma a member of the Church of Christ, Marian Guinn, was engaged in an illicit relationship with a man in the community. She was called in by the church elders, told that she must publicly repent and mend her ways, and that if she refused the church would separate her from fellowship.

Guinn refused; so the elders presented her case to the church, which separated her from fellowship.

Guinn in turn hired a lawyer, who sued the church for $1.3 million, arguing that, "It doesn't matter if she was fornicating up and down the street. It doesn't give [the church] the right to stick their noses in."

Incredibly, or so it seems to me, the court took jurisdiction. The case was decided in Guinn's favor; the church was held liable for "invading her privacy"!

That is the most outrageous and dangerous intrusion into the affairs of the church ever. The state is saying that holiness—requiring church members to live by biblical standards—is not the business of the church.

What a travesty! A nation which is

attempting to restore prayer to its schools is at the same time rejecting holiness in its churches. If the Guinn case is sustained on appeal, the church will, in fact and in law, be reduced to nothing more than a Sunday morning Rotary Club.

Fifth, evangelism is more than proclamation; it is demonstration. We live in an age of deep skepticism. Most surveys reveal that people do not believe what they see and hear through the media. (Perhaps we can be grateful for that.) Public respect for institutions and professions has steadily declined. Ministers do a little better in public opinion polls than politicians, but that is not saying much.

There are few people, at least in the Western world, who have not *heard* the Gospel message. So we have to conclude that countless millions either reject it, do not apply it to themselves, or do not regard it as relevant. There are also millions who will never cross the threshold of our churches; as many churches flee the inner cities and head for the high ground of the suburbs, they leave behind people who simply do not feel comfortable enough—or good enough—to come into our handsome sanctuaries.

How then do we break through this cultural barrier and overcome the skepticism and distrust levied toward evangelicals? Surely that is a priority for us.

The answer lies in obedience. The gritty and sacrificial type that we sometimes, amid our comfortable and cloistered lifestyles, never even consider. But when we Christians take the biblical message to heart and have the courage *to live in obedience to Christ's radical commands,* we are compelled not only to preach the Gospel, but to take it into the world and live it out. Let me give you one example.

Jefferson City is a sleepy town of 30,000 people, the capital of Missouri.

It is also the site of four state penitentiaries. Most of the inmates come from Kansas City and St. Louis, several hundred miles away.

Every weekend the wives, children, and families of inmates descend on Jefferson City to visit their loved ones in prison. Most can't afford a motel, and are forced to sleep in cars or parking lots or on park benches. There have been some very unfortunate incidents over the years because of the situation.

A few years ago, Prison Fellowship volunteers saw the needs of these unwanted visitors. They began to invite inmates' families into their homes. That became difficult to manage, however, so a small committee was formed, and an old boarding house located. Volunteers from 12 local churches raised $46,000, bought the home, and with volunteer manpower and contributions, restored it. The sparkling, renovated home officially opened in 1981. Its

name? Agape House. And since
November 1981 tens of thousands of
guests have passed through its doors.

Any night of the week, you will
find Agape House full of the wives,
children, fathers, and mothers of
inmates, who, for $3 a night, get a clean
bed, a Bible, and best of all, a day
care center so children can be cared
for while their parents have
uninterrupted time together. And one
of the most exciting things about
Agape House is that it is run by a
former Catholic nun and a Southern
Baptist missionary.

In my book *Loving God,* I tell the
story of their powerful ministry
through the example of a woman I'll
call Sherry.

Sherry, who knew the underside of
life, worked in a bar, clinging to the
thin hope that her husband,
sentenced for life, would be released.
One evening she was sitting at Agape
House's dining room table listening to
other prison widows, when the two

women of God who manage Agape House came through the room, dispensing towels, asking about husbands, stopping to admire a small child's toy.

Sherry turned away from the conversation and mused, "I don't even know if there is a God. But if He is real and He is good, He must be something like these ladies at Agape House."

You see, my friends, that is not waiting for people to come into our churches or listen to our sermons on radio and television. That is taking the Gospel to them where they are, sharing in their suffering at their point of need, letting them *see* the Good News lived out through God's people.

And when we do this, the world pays attention. Not only does a hardened prisoner's wife like Sherry come to realize that there is a God, but even the secular world can see the difference we Christians make living out our faith. Agape House was even singled out by President Reagan for national recognition in 1982—as an example to the world of what needs to be done in our communities.

The secular world sees the same thing every time our ministry conducts a community service project—when we take inmates out of prison for two weeks to help the needy, like the project that renovated the home of an elderly Atlanta widow; or the San Antonio project with Habitat for Humanity that built a house for a Spanish-speaking couple with six foster children; or the inmates in Columbia, South Carolina who refurbished an inner city playground just before Christmas.

Prison Fellowship is doing these projects all over the country, and each time we do, the secular media sits up and takes notice. They might not cover our church services, but they'll turn out when we invade their territory and make a difference in peoples' lives where they live. The Good News needs to be *seen* as well as heard.

A *Future of Promise*

What then is our challenge in the decades ahead?

How do we fulfill our biblical commission in an age of unbelief—when orthodoxy is unconsciousness?

1. By being witnesses with the totality of our lives;

2. By discipling others, one-on-one; not just making converts, but training them to live disciplined, holy lives;

3. By breaking out of our comfortable cocoons and engaging the secular world in battle for the hearts and minds of our culture;

4. By strengthening the role of the church, making it truly a holy community; and

5. By taking the Gospel into a hostile, skeptical world, living it out for all to see.

An awesome challenge? Yes, indeed. But if God is for us, who can be against us? We, who know a God who is sovereign and at work in history, have no cause for timidity, but have the spirit of "power, love, and a sound mind," as the Apostle Paul wrote to Timothy. We are called to be obedient to One whose will cannot be thwarted.

C.C. Goen, the eminent church historian, wrote of the Reformed tradition, "It bred a race of heroes willing to topple tyrants, carve new kingdoms out of howling wilderness, and erect holy commonwealths to fulfill the righteousness of God on earth."

Let us be about our business, my brothers and sisters, that we might be found worthy of this, our heritage— and our sovereign Lord's mission for us.